WORLD MYTHS AND LEGENDS II

Mexico

Flora Foss

Fearon/Janus/Quercus
Belmont, CA

Simon & Schuster Education Group

World Myths and Legends

Greek and Roman
Ancient Middle Eastern
Norse
African
Far Eastern
Celtic
Native American
Regional American

World Myths and Legends II

India
Russia
Europe
South America
The Caribbean
Central America
Mexico
Southeast Asia

Series Editor: Joseph T. Curran
Cover Designer: Dianne Platner
Text Designer: Teresa A. Holden
Interior Illustrations: Carol Stutz
Cover Photo: The Granger Collection, New York

Library of Congress Catalog Card Number: 92–72301
ISBN 0–8224–4632–4
Printed in the United States of America
2. 10 9 8 7 6 5 4 3 2 1
EB

CONTENTS

4　Heroes, Tricksters, and Rascals

An Introduction to the Myths and Legends of Mexico

Spanish explorers landed in Mexico in the 1500s. There they found people with an advanced civilization. These people had built beautiful cities, great temples, and pyramids. They cultivated crops and wove cloth. They had busy markets in which many kinds of goods were sold.

The Spanish explorers found stunning art and architecture in this sunny land. The native people had developed a picture system of writing and a complex calendar. Their religion was highly developed.

These flourishing cultures belonged to the Maya and the Aztec peoples. Other tribes also lived in Mexico. All of them may have grown out of the earlier civilization of the Olmec people, who lived around 2200 B.C.

The Mexican natives had a rich body of myths and legends. Stories were told from generation to generation. They were a way of sharing and passing on an understanding of how the world works.

The tellers of these stories were often giving an education to young people. Myths and legends were told by a storyteller and an assistant. The assistant made comments and asked questions. This method made the stories seem like conversations.

Some ancient stories were sacred. These myths were based on beliefs about the spiritual world. They told how the world, its people, and its animals were created. They explained how the heavens and the earth worked.

These ancient stories expressed a sense of mystery and power. They awakened deep within people an awareness of the miracles of birth, growth, and death. They echoed the cycles that rule people's lives and their planet.

The Indian tribes of Mexico recognized various gods, but their myths all pointed to one supreme being. This supreme being was the source of the gods who directly affected the earth. The gods of sun, moon, wind, earth, crops, rain, birth, and death were believed to take direct actions on the earth. People saw and felt their effects. Myths about these gods were told to give order to the world.

Other stories, which came later, were told to pass along the people's way of looking at life. They illustrated what was needed to live in harmony with the world. They told of adventurers, heroes, and evildoers. Animals are characters in many of the tales. These animals speak and act like people. The animals usually stand for people's good and bad qualities. In such legends, people, animals, and gods alike may have magic powers.

These stories are often humorous and entertaining. However, they also pass along the people's sense of right and wrong. They show what is to be valued. They give life to people's deepest wishes, hopes, and fears. They sometimes laugh at human weaknesses and cry for life's hard realities.

Many tribal people still live in Mexico. The Yaqui, Seri, Popoluca, Mazatec, Tzotzil, and Zapotecans are a few of these tribes. A number of them are descended from the ancient Maya and Aztecs.

Many of these people have kept alive a tradition of myths and legends. Ancient beliefs, history, and current concerns are combined in these stories. Also, tales and customs brought to Mexico by the Spanish have been worked into the native stories. Incidents that deal with social issues appear in some stories. These myths and legends are kept vital to the people. They represent the rich and varied heritage of Mexico.

How the Gods Made People

There is an ancient Mayan book called Popol Vuh. *In it is this story of how the world and its people were made.*

In the beginning, only the heavens and the waters existed. There was no earth, and there were no living things. Everywhere there was silence and darkness. Only the gods shone with dazzling brightness.

The gods got together and made a decision. The earth was to appear, flat like a plate. Light would fill the skies. These things came to be.

At first there were only clouds on the new earth. Then land rose from the waters, and forests and flowers grew. Later the gods made animals to live on the earth.

Even with animals, however, the world was still silent. The gods commanded the animals, "Speak! Say our names and worship us, because we are your father and mother."

A terrible hissing, bellowing, and cackling noise came out. Since the animals had no language, they could not say their makers' names. The animals could not say words.

Sadly the gods told them, "You cannot worship us. You will be made to obey and to be food for those who come after you."

The gods talked with one another again. How could they make creatures who could be able to know and worship them? They scooped up some earth, spat life into it, and formed creatures of clay.

Now these clay people could not stand up straight. They had heads that were full of clay, and they could not think. When they tried to talk, out came nonsense, not words.

The gods were not pleased. They knew this creation would not last. The clay people would melt in the water. Sure enough, when it rained, the clay people melted away.

The gods talked together yet another time. They asked, "What can we do to form people who will understand us and who will worship us?"

After much discussion, the gods decided to make people out of wood. Quickly, before the new dawn came, they made wooden people and gave them life.

The people of wood walked and talked and had children, who were also wooden. Because the wooden people had no blood, they had nothing in their hearts or heads.

They also forgot their makers, so the gods sent a flood to destroy them. A sticky rain covered the earth. The animals and even the pots and pans and plates rose up against the wooden people. The wooden people fled. They climbed to their roofs, but their houses fell. They climbed up trees, but the trees threw them off. They looked for shelter in caves, but the caves closed up their mouths. The wooden people were washed away.

A few survived. They were turned into monkeys and had to live in trees. They were left as a sign of this failed creation.

Then there was just a trace of early dawn, but no sun. The earth lay in darkness. The gods met yet once again. Clay and wood had not been good dwellings for the spirits of humans. Soon dawn would come, and their creation should be finished by then. The gods sent prayers into the night.

Then the fox, the coyote, the parrot, and the crow came and told the gods about a special food called maize, or corn. The ears of maize could form the flesh and blood of people.

The gods made four men out of the maize. These were the children of the gods. The gods spat life into the men, and then they watched.

Before their eyes sprang tall, brown, handsome people. When they talked and thought and walked about and touched things, the men were seeing and feeling. They built houses from clay and wood. They worked in the fields and hunted for food.

These four men saw everything perfectly. They understood what was on the earth and in the heavens. They praised their creators with a glorious musical sound.

"We live because of the gods," the men praised. "You have given us everything. Because of you we speak, hear, move, and feel. Thank you, our makers, for giving us life. Thank you, our ancestors, for letting us see both the far and the near. We give thanks, for we understand all that is in heaven and all that is on earth."

The gods started to worry. The men they had created knew too much. So the gods met one last time.

"Won't these men want to be as we are?" the gods asked. "We have given them too much vision."

So the gods blew mist into the eyes of the men. Their sight was clouded as though a mirror might be fogged by breath. The men could no longer see everything clearly. This is as it is even today.

Then the gods formed women. When the men saw the women, their hearts filled with joy because they were no longer alone.

These men and women became the ancestors of all the tribes. The gods were very satisfied, and they rejoiced in their creation.

1. *Why were the animals not pleasing to the gods?*
2. *What happened to a few of the wooden people?*
3. *What did the gods use to make human beings?*

The Legend of the Five Suns

> In this Aztec creation story, the conflict between two gods causes the destruction of the world four different times. Quetzalcoatl is the most powerful figure in all the Mexican myths and legends. His greatest enemy is Tezcatlipoca. The two gods take different forms as they battle each other. Four different suns and four different races of people are wiped out by the continual fighting of this pair.

The Tiger Sun

In the beginning, there was no sun and no people. Only the gods lived in the sky. They wanted to create light so that the world might have life. They also wanted to create people.

The gods Quetzalcoatl and Tezcatlipoca were always fighting. Quetzalcoatl wanted only good things for creation. Tezcatlipoca, who could take many forms, worked only for evil. So the two were always competing.

There have been four great eras before the one we now live in. The first great era was the age of the Tiger Sun. This is how it began. Tezcatlipoca, as god of night, changed himself into a tiger. His spotted skin filled the sky with stars. Then he made himself into the Tiger Sun, and the world was lit.

The gods made the first race of people, who were giants. These beings lived like wild animals. They didn't till the soil or plant crops but wandered about and ate whatever plants they could find.

Quetzalcoatl searched for his enemy Tezcatlipoca. He took his great club and knocked the tiger down into the waters below. Since Tezcatlipoca was the sun, the earth became dark. Then Tezcatlipoca became very angry. He climbed up onto the land and ate up the giants. Tezcatlipoca remained on earth waiting to take his revenge on Quetzalcoatl.

The first great age had ended.

The Sun of Air

Quetzalcoatl made himself into the second sun. He took the form of wind and was known as the Sun of Air. He shone over the second race of people. Animal instinct had reigned the first age, but pure spirit

The Tiger Sun

reigned in the second age. However, the people of this age were not ready for pure spirit. Tezcatlipoca knew this. He watched and waited.

One day Tezcatlipoca stretched a great tiger paw into the heavens when the Sun of Air wasn't looking. The god came tumbling down to earth. A terrible hurricane began. Everything that grew was torn up by the roots. The fall killed almost all the people. Only a few survived, and these were turned into monkeys.

The second great age had ended.

The Sun of the Rain of Fire and the Sun of Water

The mother and father of the gods were displeased. They made Quetzalcoatl and Tezcatlipoca leave the sky. Then they made a third sun to burn in the sky. It shone over the third race of beings.

The third creation was all wrong from the start. Quetzalcoatl returned and burned it in a rain of fire. Of course, the people were burned, too. Those that did not die were turned into birds and flew to a safe place.

The third great age had ended.

Then Quetzalcoatl spoke to Lady Precious

Green, the storm goddess. He convinced her to be the fourth sun, the Sun of Water. For a while, Lady Precious Green shone on the earth and on the fourth race of people.

Then Tezcatlipoca caused a great flood to cover the earth. The people of the Sun of Water drowned except for some who were turned into fish.

The fourth great age had ended.

The Tiger Sun had been all strength, and he had failed. The Sun of Air had been all spirit, and he had failed, too. Neither the Sun of the Rain of Fire nor the Sun of Water had been able to keep life going on the earth. Still, there had to be creation. The gods wondered what they should do next.

The Sun of Movement

The gods looked down and saw that the flood that Tezcatlipoca had sent had completely covered the earth. The sky itself was filled with water. They sent Quetzalcoatl and Tezcatlipoca to lift the waterlogged sky from the earth.

The gods were sad when they saw that the sun had been destroyed. There must be light for their fifth creation. A new sun was needed. They decided that the new sun would have to be one that moved.

The gods met and discussed what should be done. All of them agreed that a sacrifice was needed to show their sorrow. One of them would jump into the spirit oven and be made pure. Only then could there be light.

One god, who was poor and ill, said, "Let me be the one."

A second god, who was rich and powerful, also volunteered. "After all," he bragged, "my offerings will be more pleasing to our father because they are more precious."

For the next four days, the two gods prepared for the lighting of the spirit oven. The rich one gave many fine gifts to the father of the gods. The poor one could only give moss and thorns that were tipped with his own blood. The gods lit the fire and tended it carefully.

On the fifth day, the blazing fire was ready. The rich god put himself first and got ready to leap into the flames. He raced forward but stopped just as he reached the edge of the oven. Three times he tried, and three times he failed.

It was the poor god's turn. Without a pause, he closed his eyes and leapt into the very heart of the fire. A shout went up all around as a great flame shot up from the spirit oven. Out of it rose the poor god. He had been made pure and changed into the sun.

The rich god's face burned with shame. The spirit-oven fire was going out. Quickly he threw himself into it. Slowly he burned in the dying embers until he, too, was pure. He was then changed into the pale moon.

The gods thought the rich god had behaved badly. They angrily threw a rabbit at the moon. You can see it there to this day, in the dark spots on the moon's face.

Then the gods turned to admire the radiant sun that had risen in the east. There it stood, quite still.

"What's wrong?" asked the puzzled gods. "Why doesn't it move on its course?"

The sun answered the gods. The sun said, "If you want me to move, you must give me your precious life's blood."

At first the gods angrily refused, but they saw that this was of no use. Unless they sacrificed themselves, the sun would not move in the heavens. So the gods did sacrifice themselves then, and they became the stars in the sky.

Then the fifth sun, called the Sun of

Movement, began to travel on its course across the sky. It blazed brilliantly along its way. The pale moon and the stars followed after it.

The light of the Sun of Movement was life-giving for the fifth race of people. Neither water, fire, air, nor earth could act alone to make life for human beings. A little of each, together with movement, brought life and balance.

This race of people were our ancestors. We still live in the age of the Sun of Movement. It, too, will be destroyed someday.

1. *How did the first great age end?*
2. *How did the poor god become the fifth sun?*
3. *What had to happen before the fifth sun could move on its course?*

The Boy Who Brought Corn

The Popoluca of the state of Vera Cruz tell this myth about a boy who brings the people corn. Corn is the most important crop, and the boy is truly a hero. However, no one understands at first why the boy has come. Before he can fulfill his purpose, he must escape many dangers and even outwit a god.

The Egg in the Water

There once lived an old couple who had no children. Every day the woman carried water from the stream to the house. One day when she knelt by the stream, the woman saw an egg in the water. She ran to her husband and cried, "I have found good fortune!"

"What is it?" he asked.

"It's an egg in the water," she replied. "Come, let's take it."

They rushed back to the stream. The astonished man did see an egg swimming in the clear water. "How will we get it?" he asked.

"This fishnet should work," the woman said. She plunged the net into the water, but

14

she could not catch the egg.

The man looked around and saw what was happening. The egg was really lying on a rock above the stream. What they saw in the water was its reflection.

"You've been deceived," he cried.

"No, really, I have found good fortune," the woman insisted.

The man climbed up the rock for the egg. Then his wife hid the egg in her clothes. She took care of it for seven days.

On the seventh day, the old couple heard crying. Looking in the wife's clothing, they found a tiny child with golden hair as soft as corn silk.

"See, I told you!" the old woman cried. "The egg has brought us good fortune."

"He'll be a son for us to raise," the old man replied happily.

A Runaway

After just seven more days, the boy had grown tall and could walk and talk. The woman sent him to the stream for water.

When the boy knelt by the stream, the minnows made fun of him. "Why, you are only a little egg that was taken from the water with a fishnet!" they jeered.

The old couple discover a child

"Don't make fun of me," the boy warned. He went and told the woman, "It makes me angry when they say I'm only an egg from the water."

The woman sent the boy back to the stream the next day. Again, the minnows made fun of him. This time he made up his mind to teach them a lesson.

"Please make me a fishhook," he asked the woman. The next time he went to the stream, he put the fishhook into the water and caught the fish. He put them into a sombrero and returned to the house to show the woman.

The woman became very upset and made the boy put the fish back. As he put the fish back into the water, he warned, "You must not make fun of me. From now on, people will seek you as food."

One day the boy went to the cornfield with the old couple. The birds began to mock him. "You're nothing but an egg," they yelled. "You're just a little egg!"

"Mother," he said, "the birds are mocking me. They are calling me an egg. I don't like what they are saying."

"Don't listen to them," she replied.

The boy couldn't stand being mocked.

"Father, please make me a bow and an arrow," he asked.

The man made the bow and the arrow. The boy didn't know that these birds were really his mother's, so he killed many of them. Soon the old woman appeared and began scolding the boy.

"You must bring the birds back to life," she insisted.

"But they mocked me!" he cried. "That's why I killed them."

The boy gave the birds back their lives, but he warned them, "Never mock me." Then he threw them into a tree.

The old man and woman were angry with the boy. It seemed he was always doing forbidden things. He didn't obey them as they thought he should.

The woman convinced her husband that they had to get rid of the boy. She said, "When he goes to bed at night, we will kill him and drink his blood."

The boy climbed up on his bed, which was a ledge hung on the wall. However, he did not go to sleep. He had heard the old people talking, and he knew they wanted to kill him. He called a bat over to him.

"When my father comes to my bed, cut his

throat," he told the bat. Then he climbed out
the window and up on the roof to wait.

At last, the woman said, "Our son sleeps."
Then the man climbed up to the ledge. Soon
the woman heard drops of blood falling. She
tasted the blood. Then she called to her
husband. He didn't answer because it was
his blood that was dripping down.

When the woman found out what had
happened, she was very angry. She called to
her son on the roof, "You killed your father.
Now I'm going to eat you."

Then the boy knew he had to run away.

No matter where he ran, the woman
followed him. No matter how far he went,
when he looked back, she was right behind
him.

"Why don't you stop, and we'll talk things
over?" she coaxed, trying to trick him.

"Leave me alone," he cried, "for I can
destroy you with my strength. I am he who is
to bring food to people."

Still the woman would not stop chasing
him. He came upon a tree in the middle of a
plain and climbed up. He knew this tree had
magic power. Just as the old woman reached
the tree, a great ring of fire sprang up
around it.

The boy called to her, "If you try to eat me, you will be burned up."

She didn't believe it, so she went right after him. The flames flickered up the tree after her and burned her to death. The boy, however, slipped through the flames without harm.

Three Jails

Now that the boy was out of danger, he traveled on to the seashore. There he made a drum and began beating on it. On the other side of the ocean, Hurakan, the wind god, heard the noise and sent one of his helpers to find out who was drumming.

The helper asked the boy, "Who are you? Tell me your name."

The boy said, "I am he who sprouts at the knees. I am he who flowers."

The helper returned to Hurakan and reported, "He didn't give me his name."

Hurakan sent the helper once again to the boy. "I must know your name," the helper said. "Hurakan wishes to know, and you must tell me."

"Very well," the boy replied. "My name is Homshuk. Tell Hurakan I am he who is shelled and eaten."

Hurakan would not believe that Homshuk was the boy's real name. He thought the boy was a *nagual*, an evil spirit in animal form. So Hurakan sent a great storm to wash Homshuk into the sea. The boy asked a tarantula to help him. "Will you build me a house," he asked, "to protect me from the rain?" The tarantula did as it was asked.

All night torrents of rain fell, but in the morning, Hurakan's men found Homshuk unharmed. He was still drumming on the shore.

Soon a big tortoise came lumbering along. It asked, "What are you doing, friend?"

Homshuk replied, "I'm here drumming, but what I really want is for you to carry me across the ocean to Hurakan. If you'll do this favor for me, I'll give you colors like no other tortoise."

The tortoise considered and then said yes. Homshuk painted the tortoise. Then he climbed upon its back and got carried across the ocean to Hurakan. Ever since, this type of tortoise has had bright colors.

Hurakan saw the boy coming. The wind god was furious, for he still believed the boy was an evil spirit.

Hurakan thought, "I know how I can get rid of him!"

He had his helpers throw the boy in a jail filled with hungry serpents. He was sure the boy was a fraud and would be eaten.

Homshuk told the serpents, "I'm strong. You must not harm me, for I must bring food to people."

The next morning Hurakan found Homshuk sitting on the largest serpent. He had sent the others to live in the woods and mountains.

The next night angry Hurakan threw Homshuk in a jail with wild tigers. He thought this time he would be rid of the boy. Homshuk told the tigers what he'd told the serpents. When morning came, the jail was empty except for Homshuk, sitting on the largest tiger.

Next, Hurakan put Homshuk in a jail that rained down arrows on him. The boy said to the arrows, "Don't hurt me. Your job is to help people defend themselves and hunt."

The arrows fell to the ground. Homshuk gathered them and sat on them. That is how Hurakan found him the next morning.

A Contest

Hurakan had failed to kill Homshuk, but still he wanted to get rid of him. So the wind god suggested a contest.

"If you win, you may live here," Hurakan said. "If I win, you must die."

"What kind of contest?" Homshuk asked.

"We'll see who can throw a stone across the ocean," Hurakan answered.

"I'm not much on throwing," the boy said, "but let me gather my own stones."

He went into the woods and called on a woodpecker for help.

The woodpecker asked, "What do you want of me?"

"If you don't help me, Hurakan will kill me," Homshuk said. "I want you to fly across the ocean. When I throw a stone, begin pecking on a tree for all you are worth."

The boy threw the first stone. Soon they heard a far-off sound, "tra-tra-tra." This was the woodpecker's sound.

"Hear that?" Homshuk asked. "My stone flew with such force that it is bouncing from tree to tree on the other side of the ocean!"

Then Hurakan threw his stone. They waited for hours, but they heard no sound. Homshuk was declared the winner.

Hurakan had lost, but still he wished to kill Homshuk. Placing a giant hammock between two trees on the shore, he tried again to get rid of the boy.

"My people and I are going to cross the ocean," Hurakan said. "We will swing across in this hammock. It's an exciting way to travel. Would you like to try it?" Huraken felt sure that Homshuk would tumble out of the hammock into the ocean.

The boy climbed into the hammock, and Hurakan blew on it to start it swinging. First the hammock swayed gently, and then it rocked vigorously. Hurakan blew harder. The hammock began swinging violently out over the water. What a rough ride Homshuk had! However, he held on with all his strength.

Finally, Hurakan stopped the hammock. The boy hopped out, a little unsteadily. He recovered quickly so that no one would notice. Now he had a trick of his own in mind.

"What a good way to cross the ocean!" Homshuk cried. "I only came back because I didn't know where you were planning to go yourself. You go ahead, and I will follow."

Puzzled, Hurakan and all his people climbed in. Meanwhile, the boy called a gopher over to him.

"Gopher," he said, "you must cut the roots of these two trees very fast."

Homshuk began to swing the hammock. Soon it was swishing out and up as far as it had before. At that time, the gopher cut the last root. Hammock, trees, and people fell into the ocean. All Hurakan's people were killed. Only Hurakan managed to escape. He made it to shore and begged Homshuk for forgiveness. He had finally decided that Homshuk was truly who he had said he was.

"I don't know if I should forgive you. What can you offer me?" Homshuk asked.

"The corn that sprouts from you must have water to live," replied Hurakan. "In the dry times, I can bring water to help the corn grow."

Homshuk agreed, for he knew that the crops would need water in June and July.

Since then, Hurakan has watered the cornfields at this time of year. Since then, the people have had corn to eat.

1. *Why did the boy have to run away from his mother?*
2. *Why did Hurakan want to kill Homshuk?*
3. *How did Homshuk finally defeat Hurakan?*

How the People Got Corn

Here is another myth explaining how corn became food for people. Here the gods' help is needed to free the corn that is hidden in a mountain.

After the gods had created people, they looked at one another and asked, "What shall the people eat?"

Quetzalcoatl knew there was corn on the earth. It was hidden inside a great rock called Corn Mountain. The problem was how the people could get the corn out.

Quetzalcoatl went to Corn Mountain and searched until he found a crack. Then he turned himself into an ant and crawled inside the rock. He was able to carry kernels of corn out through the crack in the rock.

Quetzalcoatl changed himself back into his god form and returned to the spirit world, carrying the corn with him. Then the gods chewed the kernels and placed them on the people's lips. In this way the people grew strong.

However, the gods didn't tell the people where to get more corn. No one on earth knew about the corn except the ants who had followed Quetzalcoatl into the rock.

The people and the animals of the earth were hungry. They had to dig for whatever roots they could find. Sometimes they also found fruit here and there. Still, they were usually hungry.

Then one day, as Fox was trotting along, he noticed something strange. He saw some white kernels on the path. Careless ants had dropped these kernels of corn as they carried them from under the rock. Fox gobbled them up. They were delicious. He wondered how he could get more of this wonderful food.

Fox hid himself in the bushes and waited. That night the ants came marching, one by one, along the path. Fox followed them all the way to the crack in the rock, where they disappeared. When Fox tried to get in, he only scratched his nose, because he was much too large.

Soon the ants filed out, carrying corn. Once again Fox ate whatever kernels the ants dropped.

The other animals noticed that Fox was getting a full belly. They gathered around him curiously. "What have you been eating?" they asked.

All they got for a reply was a loud burp. Again they asked, "What have you been eating? Your breath smells so sweet." "Oh, nothing much," Fox replied. "I just ate a few roots." The other animals didn't believe him. When Fox went to bed, they met and agreed to follow him the next day.

The next morning Fox left his home for Corn Mountain. The other animals were keeping themselves hidden behind bushes and trees. They saw him as he waited for the ants and began to eat the corn. Then the animals jumped out. "Aha!" they cried. "We knew you were eating something different! Let us try it."

There was nothing Fox could do but say yes. All the animals tried a little corn and liked it. They decided to wait for the ants and ask them to share the corn.

The ants listened. They agreed to bring corn to the hungry animals. They began carrying the corn out of the crack. Before long it became clear that the animals would never be satisfied. A kernel of corn is a lot to an ant. To a large animal, it is not even a bite.

At last the tired ants cried, "Enough! We

can't keep this up. From now on, we will only bring out food for ourselves."

What could the animals do? They tried everything, but only the ants were small enough to get inside Corn Mountain. At last the animals went to the people and told them about the new food. The people decided to ask the Thunder Lords for help.

Old Man Lightning, the greatest of the Thunder Lords was nowhere to be found. However, the people found three young Thunder Lords who were willing to try to break the rock open. These three raced to the rock and threw their lightning bolts against it. What a disappointment! The rock didn't break at all.

Old Man Lightning was secretly watching all the while. When the young Thunder Lords sent word to him, he kept himself hidden. Again they sent a messenger. This time Old Man Lightning replied, "I'm an old man. If the strong young ones cannot split the rock, how can I?"

A final time the young Thunder Lords sent a message. "We have tried and we have failed," it said. "We cannot break the rock."

Then Old Man Lightning was satisfied and came out to help the Thunder Lords. He called to Woodpecker, "Fly over there and tap the rock with your beak. Find the place where it sounds the thinnest. In that place, it will be hollow underneath. That is where the corn must be hidden."

Woodpecker flew to the mountainside, and tap-tap-tap he went over the rock. At last he showed Old Man Lightning the thinnest place.

"Good!" he said. "That is where my thunderbolt will fly. You must hide yourself now, my woodpecker, or the lightning will kill you."

Woodpecker hid behind a ledge. Then Old Man Lightning gathered all his strength and threw his bolt of lightning against the rock. When the lightning struck the rock, a great boom was heard, and the rock shattered.

The noise startled Woodpecker so much that he forgot to keep hidden and stuck his head out. A piece of rock struck his head, and blood soon covered the top of it. From that time on, Woodpecker has had a red spot on the top of his head.

The corn came pouring out, roaring like a mighty river. Inside the rock all the corn had been white. When the thunderbolt hit, it burned some of the corn, turning it red.

Woodpecker helps Old Man Lightning

Smoke colored other kernels, making them yellow.

The three young Thunder Lords took the white corn and planted it. Old Man Lightning planted the yellow corn and the red corn.

There was now plenty of food for all the people and all the animals on earth.

1. *Who was able to get into Corn Mountain first?*
2. *Why did the animals need to ask the people for help?*
3. *How did Woodpecker and Old Man Lightning get the corn out?*

Possum Steals Fire

The Mazatec live in the state of Oaxaca. They tell this myth about the animal hero who brings fire to the people.

At one time fire existed only on certain stars and planets in the heavens. One day some fire fell to earth, and an old woman saw it. She was fearless and rushed to get the fallen fire. She managed to keep it going. However, she kept it only for herself.

After a long time, the people began to grumble. "Fire should be for everyone," they said. "Why should she alone have it? It isn't right!"

So the people went to the woman's house and asked for some fire. Not only did the woman say no, but she was as fierce as a tiger! She wouldn't give fire to anyone, and she turned the people away.

The people were cold because they had no fire. They longed to have fire for keeping warm and for cooking their food.

As time went on, the old woman managed to keep the wonderful fire, but she still refused to share it. Possum heard about the

situation and went to talk to the people.
"I, Possum, can get fire for you," he said.
"I promise to bring fire and to share it with
all of you. In return, you must promise never
to hunt and eat me."
The people nearly fell all over themselves
laughing. How could Possum do what they
themselves had been unable to do? They
made fun of the poor animal. Possum,
however, wasn't ruffled a bit. He remained
calm. In answer to their jokes and insults, he
just said, "If you make fun of me, you are
only mocking yourselves. You must stop.
Wait and see. This very night you'll see how I
keep my promise."
When evening fell, Possum traveled from
house to house. At each house he visited, he
told the people he was going to get fire from
the old woman and bring it to as many
people as he could.
Finally he arrived at the old woman's
house. "A pleasant good evening," he said to
her. "Brrr. It's freezing out here. Could I
come in and stand next to your fire for a
minute to get warm? This cold will be the
death of me!"
The old woman believed Possum.
Thinking he only wanted to warm himself,

she permitted him to come into her house. He went near the fire, then nearer, and then nearer still.

Clever Possum! At last he was so near the fire that he could put his tail right into it. That is just what he did.

Then with his tail ablaze, Possum ran swiftly from the old woman's house. He stopped at the nearest house, where the people waited with wooden sticks. He touched the sticks with his tail. Soon the people had a blazing fire by which to warm themselves.

Possum ran on from house to house. He ran as far as he could, sharing the fire. The beautiful hair on his tail burned completely away.

That is why, to this day, the possum has a bald tail.

1. *Where did the old woman get fire?*
2. *What did Possum tell the old woman he wanted to do?*
3. *How did Possum get fire from the old woman?*

Possum shares the fire

Why the Sun Is So High in the Heavens

The Huichols live in the Western Sierra Madre, a chain of mountains in the states of Nayarit and Jalisco. The Huichols tell this story to explain why the sun once lived close to the earth and why it moved far away.

The Huichols lived in the mountains. They farmed on the rugged slopes and hunted wild turkeys.

The people loved and respected the sun, for a god lived within it.

"What shall we call the sun?" they asked.

"I know," a little boy said. "The call of the wild turkey that greets the rising sun is beautiful. The turkey is like the sun, for it has been given to help us live."

The wild turkey's call went "Shoé-pi-tou-tou-tou." So the Huichols called the sun Tou.

The Huichols would have been content with their way of life except for one problem. Their beloved sun was too close to the earth. Tou was lonely and wanted to be close to the people of the earth.

Because the sun was so close, the earth

became hotter and hotter. People, animals, and crops were being burned up. The people wanted Tou to go high into the sky, but Tou could not bear to live far from the earth.

The boy who named the sun had an idea. He said, "I'll go with you, Tou, if you will travel higher in the sky."

So Tou agreed. Tou rose higher in the sky, taking the boy with him. In a little while, Tou stopped and asked the people, "Will this do?"

"No," the people replied. "It is still too hot. Go higher."

So Tou rose higher yet in the sky, taking the boy with him. Again he asked, "Is this far enough?" Again the people told him to go even higher, for it was still too hot.

Three more times Tou stopped, and each time the people told him to go higher. On the last time, the people finally said to Tou, "That is just right. You should be just that high in the sky."

The sun was content to remain there. The boy was with it, and so it no longer felt lonely. The people were content, too, for the earth was no longer burning hot.

Ever since, the sun has remained at just the right distance from the earth. It gives the

Tou heats the earth

people pleasant light and warmth instead of burning them up. It helps the plants grow. For these things, the people give the sun thanks and praise.

1. *Why did the sun once live much closer to the earth?*
2. *For what sound was the sun named?*
3. *Why did the people ask the sun to move?*

The Warrior and the Princess

Two famous volcanoes lie close together in the state of Pueblo. They are in the mountains that circle the Valley of Mexico. One is named Ixtlaccihuatl, which means "The White Woman." The other volcano is called Popocatepetl, which means "Smoking Mountain." For centuries this volcano has periodically spewed out smoke.

Long ago, the Aztecs nicknamed the volcanoes Ixtla and Popo. They told this story about how they came to be.

There once was an Aztec emperor who was both powerful and wealthy. He was able to keep all enemies out of his kingdom.

The emperor lived in splendor, but what he prized most was his only child. This daughter, named Ixtlaccihuatl, was beautiful and lively and had many friends. Everyone called her Ixtla.

As Ixtla grew to be a young woman, the emperor saw to it that she learned the duties of a ruler. He wanted her to follow him on the throne. There was no one else he loved and trusted as much. Ixtla was an obedient girl, so she studied hard to learn how to rule well.

Then something happened that the emperor hadn't counted on. Ixtla fell in love with Popocatepetl, a brave warrior who worked for her father. Popo, as he was called, loved Ixtla just as much as she loved him.

Only one thing stood in the way of their happiness. The emperor had forbidden his daughter to marry anyone. He thought she would be a stronger ruler if she sat on the throne alone. For years Popo and Ixtla begged him to allow them to marry, but he never changed his mind.

As the emperor grew old and weak, he could no longer lead his warriors into battle. His enemies understood his weakness and waged war against him. They battled him fiercely, hoping to take his kingdom.

The emperor called around him the best and bravest of his warriors. He wanted them to fight long and hard. He needed to give them a good reason to do so.

"The war will be long," he said sadly. "Rivers of blood will be shed. To the warrior who can crush my enemies, I will give my throne. I will also give the hand of my only daughter."

Every warrior wanted to win, so they

went to battle ready to fight long and hard. They were fighting not only to protect their homeland. They also were fighting for a beautiful bride and great power and wealth. When Ixtla heard what her father had offered the warriors, her heart sank. She wanted to marry Popo and no one else.

The war was long and bloody. The warriors fought fiercely, but none fought harder or more bravely than Popo. Armed with his shield and club, Popo showed great bravery and leadership. He led the final charge of the warriors. The enemy fled from them.

The warriors had to agree that Popo, as leader of the victory, deserved the reward. Now he could go home in triumph to claim his throne and his bride.

Not all the warriors were happy for Popo. Some were jealous. Since they could not win the rewards, they planned to destroy his happiness. These rivals slipped away from the others and raced back to the emperor.

They told the emperor that although the war was won, Popo had been killed and his body was lost.

As soon as Ixtla heard the news, she went to her room and lay down. Everyone could

Ixtla hears of Popo's death

see she was quite ill. The emperor sent for his doctors and priests, but no one could make the princess well. Her illness had no name unless it was a broken heart. Ixtla did not want to live without Popo. She faded as a flower does, and soon she died.

The day after Ixtla died, Popo returned to the emperor's palace. Before a huge, cheering crowd, the emperor greeted him.

"Welcome, my son!" the emperor said. "Here is my crown. You deserve to wear it."

Popo refused the crown. "First I must see Ixtla," he said.

Popo asked that they be married at once. Then it was his wish that Ixtla be crowned empress when he was crowned emperor. Only then did the old emperor tell Popo that Ixtla had died.

The victory meant nothing to Popo without Ixtla. His grief was so great that nothing could relieve it.

Popo found out about the liars who had told the emperor that he had died. Without a word, Popo took his warriors and went to find the jealous liars. He challenged each one to fight him. He defeated and killed them one by one. Then he gently carried Ixtla's body far from the city. His warriors followed him.

Popo had his warriors built a great pyramid of stones. As the sun set, he climbed it and laid Ixtla's body on top. That night he slept beside the woman he had loved.

The next morning Popo said to his warriors, "Build a second pyramid close to this one and a little higher. Tell the emperor that I will never rule. I will stand watch over the princess's grave."

These were Popo's last words. When the second pyramid was finished, he climbed to the top, carrying a torch. Popo stood there, with the torch held high.

The warriors below saw white smoke rising. As the sun set behind the pyramid, the smoke turned pink, then blood red.

Popo stood there faithfully the rest of his years, holding the torch in memory of Ixtla. In time, the pyramids became snow-capped mountains. People still admire their lofty beauty.

There is still evidence that the fire burns. Sometimes smoke pours out of Popo's mountain. When people see the smoke, they remember the love of the brave warrior and the beautiful princess.

1. *Why wouldn't the emperor let Popo and Ixtla marry?*
2. *What happened to Ixtla when she heard Popo had been killed?*
3. *Why did Popo climb to the pyramid with his torch?*

The Big Race

A basilisk is a kind of lizard that lives near rivers. The people of the state of Quintana Roo tell this story. It explains how the basilisk got the crest on his head and back.

The Lord of the Woods decided to hold a contest. He gathered all the animals together at the edge of the woods. A large field lay there. In the middle of the field stood a tree.

He said, "My children, I want to see which of you can reach that tree over there first. I have put a bench under the tree. Whoever arrives first is to sit on the bench. The winner of the race will get a fine prize."

The first to speak up was Fox. "My Lord," he said, "you know very well that none of us is a match for Big Deer. He is the swiftest runner, for he has the most powerful legs. Why, he flies like a windstorm!"

"Yes, it is true," added Rabbit. "None of us could hope to defeat Big Deer."

All the animals agreed. No one wanted to try to beat Big Deer to the bench.

Basilisk had been listening from his place in the branches of a bush. Now the young lizard slipped down and asked the Lord of the Woods, "My Lord, what prize will you give to the winner?"

"I will place a sombrero on the winner's head," he said. "If you win, my little friend, from then on everyone will know you have beaten Big Deer in a race."

The other animals had been listening. They began to howl with laughter. "What are you thinking of?" they asked. "You must be out of your mind. A weak little creature like you hasn't got a chance. It's ridiculous!"

They shook their heads and continued to make fun of Basilisk. He grew angry and said to them, "What are you laughing for? None of you has the courage to race Big Deer. You don't think much of me, but at least I'm not afraid to try. All you see of me is my smallness. Being big isn't everything!"

To the Lord of the Woods, Basilisk said, "I'd like to try. Then we'll see if I'm worthy of your fine sombrero."

The animals still hooted and scorned Basilisk. "Look at you," they said. "Just look how scrawny you are."

The Lord of the Woods smiled at Basilisk and nodded. He interrupted the animals sternly, "Be quiet, all of you."

The Lord of the Woods had Big Deer stand at the starting place. Basilisk lined up next to him.

"May I make one simple request?" the little creature asked.

"Yes. What is it?" the Lord of the Woods asked.

"When we are ready to take off, will you make everyone close their eyes for a moment?"

The Lord of the Woods agreed. He said to the animals, "On the count of three, all of you will close your eyes. At the same time, the race will start. After the race has begun, you may open your eyes. Ready? One, two, three." So the race began.

After the animals had opened their eyes, all that they could see was a big cloud of dust. Even the Lord of the Woods had vanished. He had flown ahead so he could see who would win the race.

Big Deer ran swiftly along for a while. Then he thought, "What's the hurry? I'm sure Basilisk is buried in my dust back there. Poor little fellow!" So he slowed to a trot and finished the race without even panting.

When Big Deer arrived at the tree, he found the Lord of the Woods waiting. Big

Deer started to sit on the bench, but he heard a small voice and jumped up.

"Watch out, Big Deer!" the voice said. "If you sit on me, you will surely mash me flat!"

Big Deer was astonished to find Basilisk already sitting on the bench. Big Deer blushed with shame. He hung his head and walked away, wondering how Basilisk had won the race.

The other animals began to arrive. When they saw Basilisk sitting on the bench, they were speechless.

The Lord of the Woods said, "Well done, my little Basilisk! Speed and size aren't everything. I admire your brains." Then he placed the sombrero on the little creature's head. They both smiled.

Only these two knew that Basilisk had reached the bench just a half second before Big Deer. Only the Lord of the Woods had seen Basilisk riding on Big Deer's tail.

To this day, Basilisk wears his prize. It is the crest on his head and back.

Basilisk wins the race

1. Why didn't most of the animals want to race?
2. Why did Basilisk ask that all the animals close their eyes at the start of the race?
3. Why did the Lord of the Woods admire Basilisk?

The Rain God's Servant

In this story, the Mayan rain god Chac takes a human boy for a servant. The results are disastrous. The plantain tree mentioned in the story bears a green, starchy fruit. It is cooked and eaten like a vegetable.

Chac, the rain god, wanted a servant. He went down to earth, stole a boy, and took him to the sky.

Chac told the boy, "Dig up some yams for me. Be careful not to look into the hole under the root."

The boy dug and pulled up the yams. "What would happen if I did look into the hole?" he thought. "There must be something really special down there that Chac doesn't want me to see."

After the boy had pulled out the very next yam, he peeked into the hole. There was the earth below him. Far away, but directly under him, was his own home. He could see his older brother. He wanted very much to go home.

"It's not so far," he said. "I can easily make it there."

The boy got a great length of rope and tied one end to a tree. He tied the other end around his middle, and little by little, he began to let himself down.

The rope was long but not nearly long enough to reach the earth. Pretty soon the boy came to the end of the rope and found himself dangling in space. He couldn't climb back up, and he couldn't jump to earth. The wind began to blow fiercely, pushing him this way and that. He was gripped with fear.

Meanwhile, Chac started to wonder what had happened to his servant. Why hadn't he come back with the yams? The rain god thundered out to the field to find him.

There was the boy, hanging onto his rope for dear life. An angry Chac hauled him up and gave him a scolding.

Plantains and Tortillas

The next day, Chac sent the boy out to gather plantains. He was hungry for the fruit of this tree.

"Cut down only the smallest trees," he warned his servant.

However, when the boy saw how small the fruit on the small trees was, he thought he would have to cut down many trees to get

Dangling in space

enough plantains.

He said to himself, "This is too much work. I can chop down just one big tree with beautiful big fruit, and my work will be done."

So he picked the biggest plantain tree he could find and started chopping. When it began to fall, it was falling in the wrong direction. It came toward him, getting bigger and bigger as it fell. There was nothing he could do. The tree fell right on top of him and trapped him under it.

This time it took many hours for Chac to miss the boy and look for him. At last he found his servant, took the tree off him, and scolded him again.

All that hard work had made the boy hungry. He remembered that Chac had told him, "My grindstone will make you tortillas."

However, in his hunger, the boy forgot something important. His master had also warned, "Never ask for more than one."

The servant called out to the grindstone without thinking, "Make me many tortillas!"

Out came huge tortillas. They fell like rain, and the boy was soon buried under them.

Once again, Chac had to rescue his servant. The rain god pulled him out and gave him the worst scolding yet.

The boy was unhappy. He longed to go home, but he thought, "A mere human shouldn't insult a god if he wants to live!"

Chac's Big Feast

The next day Chac planned a feast and invited many guests. He told the boy to clean up the house and make the table and chairs ready. The boy went to work with his broom and soon had the place sparkling for the feast.

Then he went out to watch for the guests. Soon, though, he came back in to check things one more time. Now he found that all the benches were covered with frogs! He angrily drove them off, muttering, "How dare you dirty the house that I cleaned so well!"

The time for the feast came and went, but no guests appeared. Then Chac arrived and asked, "Have my guests and musicians come?"

"Not one!" the boy replied. "All I found was a bunch of frogs dirtying up the clean house. I threw them right out."

"Aiii!" Chac exclaimed. "Those frogs were my guests and musicians! You've made another mess of things!"

The poor servant was by now very discouraged as well as homesick. Everything he had done was wrong!

The Servant's Last Adventure

Still grumbling about his spoiled feast, Chac went off to take a nap. The boy wondered what he should do next. As he was sitting in Chac's house, he saw that the rain god had left his tools out. They were a bag full of wind, a gourd of water, and a drum. Chac used them to make storms.

The servant thought, "It looks easy enough. I'll bet it's a job I can do well." He decided to take the rain god's tools and make a storm for his home on earth.

The boy stole his sleeping master's clothes and his tools. When he opened the bag, the winds went howling off. The boy wasn't nearly as strong as Chac, and he couldn't force them back into the bag. The winds screeched down on the world, starting a horrible storm.

Next the boy picked up the gourd and prepared to make rain. He didn't know that Chac made a downpour by measuring out just four fingers of water. Instead, the boy spilled out the whole gourd. A huge flood immediately poured out onto the earth.

"Hmmm," he said. "That doesn't seem quite right. Oh, well, I'll make some thunder."

Then he began beating on Chac's drum. When he wanted the drum to stop, it would not. Frantically the servant went from bag to gourd to drum, trying to stop the wind, the rain, and the thunder. He couldn't do it.

When Chac woke up, he saw that his things were gone and that his servant was missing. The master quickly got one of his helpers to lend him clothes and another bag. Then he went about stuffing the winds into the bag, calming the thunder, and stopping the rain. When he had finished, he looked for the boy.

After a long while, Chac found his servant. The strongest of all the winds, the fierce north wind, had broken him into bits. Chac passed his hands over the broken body nine times. The boy became whole and alive again.

The master took his servant back home once more, but it was for the last time.

"Boy," he said, "you can no longer stay here. When you dig yams, you wind up hanging in space. When you gather plantains, you get trapped. When you ask for tortillas, you get buried. When you prepare the house for guests, you insult them and drive them off. When I'm sleeping, you try to do a god's job and make a terrible mess. You're nothing but trouble, and I'm taking you back to earth!"

The boy smiled, for that was just what he wanted. Chac was as good as his word. He took the boy back to earth and returned to the sky.

Chac could see the boy below, playing happily with his brother. The rain god thought, "Humans belong on earth. Never again will I take one as a servant."

1. *What happened when the boy used a rope to try to reach the earth?*
2. *What were the guests and musicians at Chac's feast?*
3. *What happened when the boy took Chac's tools?*

The Animal Master's Visit

Some people of southern Mexico believe in an earth spirit known as the animal master. The spirit controls the supply of animals that humans hunt. If a hunter causes animals needless suffering, the animal master may prevent the hunter from finding more animals.

The Chinantec of the state of Oaxaca tell this story. In it, the animal master appears as a charro, or cowboy.

There was once a hunter who never had enough of shooting animals. Every day he would take his gun and go out to hunt.

This hunter shot at everything that moved. Many times he didn't even pick up all the game that he had shot. Sometimes he didn't even know whether he had hit an animal or not.

One day when he was out shooting, the hunter was approached by a man on horseback. This man was wearing the spurs and big hat of a charro.

"Sir," the charro called to him, "what do you think you're doing?"

The hunter meets the charro

"Why, I'm shooting," the hunter replied.

"Follow me," the man on horseback said.

Immediately, as though he were dreaming, the hunter found himself in a big cave with the charro. All around them were animals. Each one was wounded in some way. There were pheasants with crippled wings and rabbits that could no longer hop. There were deer with broken legs and foxes dragging their bloody tails. There were many other hurt animals as well. All of them looked at the hunter with dark, sad eyes.

"These are the animals that you have wounded," said the charro. "Do you see how much pain you have caused them? This isn't how it was meant to be. If you hunt, you must not wound the animal. You must kill it cleanly and use its flesh for food. If you don't, I'll set my two big dogs on you, and they'll eat you alive."

Suddenly the charro and the cave and its animals disappeared. The hunter then knew that he had been visited by the animal master. The hunter returned to his village. He never killed another animal.

1. What did the hunter see in the cave?
2. What did the charro tell the hunter?
3. Who did the charro turn out to be?

Three Brothers, a Toad, and a Bride

In the state of Yucatan, where this story is told, good farmland is rare. A farmer's fields may lie far from the farmer's home, and hard work is needed to raise crops. Farmers protect their farmlands vigorously. In this story, a farmer wants very much to catch a cornfield thief. One of his sons does catch the thief. The son receives magical help because of his good heart and clear thinking.

There was once a rich farmer who had three sons. He also had a fine cornfield. One day the farmer noticed that an animal had devoured the corn. He returned to the field often after that to try to discover the thief. However, he never saw who was doing the damage.

Finally, the farmer said to his sons, "One of you must bring me this creature, or I will be ruined. It may be dead or alive. I will give all that I have to whoever brings it to me."

Each of the sons wanted to earn this reward. With such wealth, anyone could have a fine life and could afford to marry.

Right away the youngest son spoke up,

"I'll bring you the creature, Father!"

"You!" mocked his older brothers. "You have neither brains nor good sense. How could you outwit this clever creature?"

"No, my son," said the father. "The oldest must try first."

The oldest son asked for a fine horse, his father's best gun, and plenty of good food. By the light of the full moon, he set out for the cornfield. Halfway there, he grew tired and stopped by a deep well to rest. A toad was croaking away nearby.

"Can't you be quiet, toad!" the young man complained. "How can I rest with your pesty noise going on?"

"Take me with you," the toad answered, "and I will tell you who is stealing your corn."

"What do *you* know? You're just a toad," he said. Without so much as a pause, he threw the toad into the water.

The young man swung up on his horse and went on his way. When he reached the field, he saw the damaged corn. However, the destroyer was nowhere to be seen. All night he kept watch, but he didn't see the thief.

By dawn the young man was very angry that he had to go home empty-handed.

"What did you see?" the father asked the young man when he got home.

The son had to admit that he had seen only the damaged corn and not the one who had damaged it.

"Then you cannot be my heir," the father said.

Next, the second oldest son tried. He asked for a gun and a bag with some food. Then he started on his way, quite sure of himself.

He, too, stopped at the well. The toad, who had pulled itself from the well, sat there croaking away. The young man wanted to rest, so he ordered the toad, "Shut up! I'm going to sleep."

"If you let me go with you," the toad said, "you won't be sorry. I can help you catch the one who is eating your corn."

"I don't need any help from you," the young man said. Then he fell asleep.

The toad became angry and ate the food from the young man's bag. When he woke up, the young man realized that the toad had eaten his food. In a fury, he grabbed the toad and threw it into the well. Still angry, he dashed away to the cornfield.

Just as he got there, he saw an amazing

sight. A huge bird with beautiful feathers was eating the corn. When it saw him, the bird flew up into the air. The son quickly raised his gun, aimed, and fired. All that fell to earth was some feathers.

He hadn't killed the bird. Even so, he thought, "I can make my father think the bird is dead." He picked up the feathers and hurried home.

When the son got home, he held the beautiful feathers up for his father and brothers to see.

"I have won!" he exclaimed. "I have killed the cornfield destroyer! Look, here are its feathers."

The youngest son frowned. "You brought feathers but not the bird that wore them," he objected. "Father, let me try! I will bring you the whole bird."

The youngest son wanted only a gun and a little food in a bag. Then he was off. Soon he, too, arrived at the well. The same little toad, who had once more pulled itself out of the water, sat there croaking away.

Walking over to it, he spoke kindly. "Little toad," he said. "can you help me? I will gladly share my food with you if you can tell me who is destroying our cornfield."

This pleased the toad. It said, "My son, your words make me happy. Your brothers, however, mistreated me and would not listen. You will enjoy the happiness that I might have given them. Here is how. At the bottom of this well lies a magic pebble. It will grant you whatever you wish."

The young man thought for a moment. His fondest wish was to find a young woman to marry. The toad's message was welcome news indeed.

"Can the pebble grant me a bride?" he asked.

"Of course," replied the toad. "It can also grant you a big wonderful house.

The young man dived to the bottom of the well and got the pebble. He wished for a bride. Then he wished for a house and to catch the cornfield thief.

The toad said, "Don't worry. It will all be as you wish."

The two of them then shared the boy's food. When they had finished eating, they started for the cornfield. As soon as they arrived there, the young man saw the bird eating the corn. The young man aimed his gun. He was about to shoot when the bird spoke in a pleasant voice.

"Please, young man, do not shoot. If you kill me, you may be killing your bride."

The young man was too surprised to move. He turned white with fear.

Again the bird spoke. "Really I'm not a bird but a woman," it said. "An old witch cast a spell on me because I wouldn't marry her son."

Suddenly the young man realized that his first wish was being granted magically. The bride he had asked for was standing before him in bird form. His happy heart gave him courage, and he spoke.

"I believe you," he said. "Let's return to my father's house. I'll ask the pebble to change you back into a woman. I'll ask my father's permission to marry you. Then, if you'll have me, we'll live in a big, beautiful house."

The bird agreed, and the young man, the toad, and the bird set out together.

Soon the father and brothers saw an amazing sight. The youngest son came into view. A toad sat on his shoulder, and a rare, beautiful bird perched on his arm.

"Here is the bird who ate our corn, Father," said the boy, "but we cannot blame her." He explained all about the toad, the

The return of the youngest son

magic pebble, and the spell cast by the witch. He finished by saying, "The toad promised that I should have a beautiful bride, and here she is."

The young man then asked the magic pebble to change the bird to her human form. Immediately, the bird vanished. In its place stood a beautiful woman. She thanked the young man for saving her and agreed to marry him.

The father rejoiced. "You have saved our cornfield," he said to his youngest son, "and you shall be my heir. You and your bride may live here as long as you wish."

Then the young man said to the pebble, "See to the building of our house."

The next morning the first rays of sun touched a dazzling, huge house. The young man and the young woman married and lived there happily. The little toad lived with them. Its croaking reminded them of the day fortune had smiled on them.

The older brothers, however, were eaten up with jealousy. They tried to harm their brother and his fine house, but all their attempts failed. Finally they ran away in disgrace, leaving their brother and his wife to live in peace.

1. *What did the older brothers do to the toad?*
2. *Who was the bird really?*
3. *What three things did the youngest brother get with the help of the toad and the pebble?*

Rosalie

This is a tale of a brave woman who helps the man she loves by using magic. The Spanish introduced this story to Mexico during the 1500s.

Four Tasks

A young man set out to make his way in the world. After he had journeyed a long time, he came upon a giant's hut. This giant had three daughters. Rosalie, the youngest one, was very beautiful. The young man quickly fell in love with her. He decided that no one but Rosalie could be his wife. As much as the young man loved her, she loved him in return.

The giant didn't really want this fellow for a son-in-law, but he said, "Very well. I will let you marry my daughter if you do just four little things for me."

"Of course," the young man replied.

"Tomorrow when I get up," the giant said, "I wish to take my bath right away. It's too far to walk to the lake, so you must bring the lake up beside my bed. Use this basket to carry it in. And mind you, have it close enough so that I can dangle my feet off the bed into the water."

The surprised young man took the basket and went to the lake. He had no idea how to complete the task. However, Rosalie had heard her father's words, and she had a plan.

"Don't worry," Rosalie said. "It shall be done."

After everyone was asleep that night, Rosalie crept out of bed and down to the lake. Using her magic skirt like a broom, she swept the lake up to her father's bed.

When the giant awoke the next morning, he couldn't believe his eyes. There was the lake water sloshing around his bedposts.

"He won't get off so easily this time," the giant muttered. He grabbed a huge jug and tossed it into the deepest part of the river. "There!" the giant roared. "Fetch me that jug from the bottom of the river. Bring it back to my hut before tomorrow morning."

The young man remembered how he loved Rosalie, and he began to dive for the jug. Again and again he dived, but he could never reach the bottom of the river. When he was ready to give up, Rosalie appeared.

"Here is what we must do," she said. "We

will return to the riverbank tonight. I will dive for the jug. When I'm at the bottom, you must say my name, or I will not be able to come up from the water."

That is just what they did. They brought the jug to the giant's hut. The next morning the first thing the waking giant saw was the jug. He marveled, but he had another task that he knew would be too hard for the young man.

The giant had to admit the young man had done well so far. "Next you must make me a cornfield in the forest," he said. "By tomorrow, you must bring me a harvest of sweet young corn from this field. Oh, and make the field exactly 100 acres."

The young man cried, "Two strong men could not clear one acre in a day!" He knew that he must first clear away all the trees and brush and get the soil ready. Then he had to plant the corn and somehow make it grow in one night.

However, for the love of Rosalie, the young man set out to work. He worked hard all day long. By the time the sun went down, however, he had not even finished clearing the field. Things looked hopeless.

Then Rosalie appeared. She stretched her

magic skirt over the forest, and all the trees fell. She used all her powers to clear the brush, plant the corn, and gather the harvest. At midnight, the young man brought Rosalie's father the tender young ears of corn.

Now the giant was furious! He stormed into his hut and asked his wife, "How can we get rid of this pesky suitor?"

She thought about it and made a plan. "I will turn myself into a horse," she said. "You will be the saddle, and Rosalie will be the bridle. Tell the young man he must bring the horse to our hut. When he gets on, I'll throw him off, and he'll be killed."

Rosalie heard every word. She wanted to use her magic to help the man she loved, not to hurt him. Still, if she disobeyed her parents, they would not let her marry. After thinking quickly, she warned the young man, "You must treat the bridle well, but have no pity on the horse and saddle." The next morning the young man asked for his final task. The giant told him that he had to travel to the woods and bring home a saddled horse that had run off.

The young man set out for the woods. The giant, his wife, and Rosalie took a shorter way. Once there, they quickly changed themselves into a horse, a saddle, and a bridle.

The young man had armed himself with a large stick. As soon as he arrived, he jumped on the horse's back and whacked it with his stick. The horse fell to the ground, without even bucking once.

The young man returned to the hut and found the giant and his wife there. They looked pretty badly beaten up.

"I have completed all four tasks," the young man said to the giant. "Now you must give me my bride."

Escape

The giant, however, had no intention of giving up his Rosalie. He told the young man there were still more tasks that had to be done. When Rosalie heard about this, she became angry.

"That's enough!" she said to the young man. "We must run away together this very night. My parents are too bruised and tired to run after us."

Rosalie waited until the giant and his wife were snoring. Then she slipped a needle, a grain of sand, and a grain of salt into her pocket. Then she spit on the floor and stole away to meet the young man.

Dawn came, and the unsuspecting giant called to his daughter, "Get up!"

"Yes, Father," Rosalie's spit said, "Don't worry, I'm already up and combing my hair." The spit sounded just like Rosalie.

However, Rosalie didn't come out of her room. The giant soon called again, "Daughter! Aren't you dressed yet? I want my breakfast."

"I'm combing my hair," came a thin whisper from the room. The spit was almost dry. The giant's wife knew something was wrong then. She discovered the trick her daughter had played.

"They have escaped!" she cried. "We've been fooled. Go after them!"

The giant ran after Rosalie and her young man. Rosalie saw her father behind her, but she knew there was more than one way out of trouble. She changed herself into an orange tree and her young man into an old man.

"Have you seen a young couple run by?" the giant asked of the old man beneath the tree.

"Nothing like that," the old man said,

"but have you ever seen such wonderful oranges? Go on, try one."

When the giant tasted an orange, he completely forgot about his anger. He went home and told his wife he could not catch the runaway couple.

"Idiot!" she cried. Her magical powers had allowed her to see what had happened far away. She knew that the orange tree was Rosalie. "Your daughter has tricked you again! Even now they are galloping away on a swift horse."

The angry giant ran after Rosalie and the young man. The earth jarred with every step. He was almost upon them when Rosalie worked her magic again. The horse became a church, the young man became a doorkeeper, and Rosalie herself became a statue.

When the giant reached the church, he asked, "Doorkeeper, have you seen a couple run by?"

"Shhh," said the doorkeeper. "Can't you have a little respect for a holy place? Look at this beautiful statue."

As soon as the giant looked at it, every thought about Rosalie went out of his head. He went back to his hut. All he could talk about was the beautiful statue he had seen.

"Numbskull!" snorted his wife. "That

statue was our Rosalie. You're perfectly useless. I see I'll have to catch them myself."
By then, Rosalie and the young man had changed back to their own forms. They ran fast, but the old woman ran faster. Closer and closer she came until she was almost upon them.
Rosalie knew there was no fooling her mother. Quick as a flash, she took the needle out of her pocket and planted it in the earth. Suddenly a thick forest grew up. While the old woman hacked her way through the forest, the young couple ran on. Before long, though, Rosalie could see the old woman gaining on them again. She reached into her pocket, drew out the grain of sand, and tossed it behind her. A huge mountain grew from the grain of sand. The old woman, huffing and puffing, scrambled up the steep slope and down the other side.
Before long the old woman had nearly caught up with the couple again. Rosalie threw down the grain of salt.
Poof! The grain of salt became an ocean. Then Rosalie turned her young man into a shark and herself into a sardine.
The old woman came wading into the water, determined to catch that sardine.

However, the shark attacked, and she had to get out.

"All right," the old woman said to Rosalie and the young man. "If you stay in the ocean for seven years, you may get married." Then she disappeared.

Return to the Village

For seven years, Rosalie and the young man swam in the ocean. Finally, they were able to return to dry land. Then they walked happily to the village of the young man's grandparents.

It was the custom of this village for visitors to bathe with holy water before entering the village. Rosalie waited just outside the village for the young man to bring her the holy water. Before he left, she gave him a warning.

"Beware," she said. "You must not touch your grandparents yet. If you do, you will forget all about me."

Of course, the old grandparents were overjoyed to see the young man. They wanted to hug and kiss him, but he wouldn't allow it.

"I'm tired," the young man thought to himself. "Surely a little nap won't hurt. Then

I'll get up and take Rosalie the holy water she needs."

So the young man fell asleep. While he slept, his grandmother tiptoed over and kissed him. Poor Rosalie! She waited many days at the edge of the village, but her young man did not come back.

Then one morning Rosalie saw a little boy playing. She asked the boy about the holy water and about her young man.

"I will bring you the water," said the boy, "but your young man is lost to you. He is going to marry someone else."

The boy brought her the holy water, and she bathed herself in it. Then she walked straight to the grandparents' hut and called to the young man. He did not remember who she was.

The young man's grandparents had arranged his marriage to another woman. It was to take place in just three days.

Rosalie had an idea. She prepared a great banquet. Then she invited everyone in the village, including the young man.

In the center of the banquet table, Rosalie placed two dolls she had made. One looked just like her. The other looked just like the young man.

When everyone was seated at the feast, Rosalie took a feather and began to tickle the man doll.

"Don't you remember how I moved the lake for you?" she cried. As she spoke, she tickled the doll's side. The young man felt a tickling in his own ribs.

"Don't you remember how I dived to the bottom of the river for you?" she said to the doll, tickling it under the chin. The young man felt a tickling under his own chin.

"What about the cornfield I made?" she asked, tickling the doll's feet. "How about the seven years we spent in the ocean?"

The young man felt a tickling from his toes to his head.

Then he cried out, "I remember, Rosalie!" Like a flood, the past came rushing back to him. With a cry of joy, he threw his arms about Rosalie.

1. *What was the first task the young man had to do for Rosalie's father?*
2. *How did the grain of salt help the young couple escape from Rosalie's mother?*
3. *Why didn't Rosalie's young man return to the edge of the village for her?*

The Cheese in the Pond

Trickster tales are very popular in Mexican folklore. A trickster is a clever character who lives by his wits. He may break the rules, but people usually admire his cleverness and his ability to overcome great odds.

The Yaqui Indians, who live in the state of Sonora, tell this story about Coyote and the trickster Fox.

Coyote was always thinking of his stomach. One evening he saw Fox sitting beside a big pond in the moonlight.

"That Fox," Coyote thought, "has played many tricks on me. Here's my chance to get even with him and fill my stomach at the same time!"

Coyote pounced upon Fox and cried out, "I'm going to eat you now!"

Fox thought quickly. He bowed his head and shook it from side to side. "Well, if you insist," he said, "but it is a great shame."

The curious Coyote asked, "What is a great shame?"

"Look in the water," Fox replied. "Do you

see the huge cheese there?"

Coyote looked, and indeed there did seem to be a huge round cheese beneath the water. However, what Coyote was actually seeing was the reflection of the full moon on the water. Coyote was letting his stomach do his thinking for him.

"It would make a fine supper," Fox said. "It's too much for me to haul out alone, and besides it's more than I can eat anyway. Why don't we work together to get it? Then we can both have a feast."

"Why not?" Coyote thought, loosening his grip on Fox. He was also thinking about having Fox for dessert after the cheese! "I can just as well eat him later as sooner," he said to himself.

"Very well," Coyote told Fox.

"Good!" Fox replied. "You stay here and keep an eye on it. I'll run and get my big fishing net. Together we should be able to scoop the cheese from the water."

Then Fox ran a little way off and hid himself in some bushes, laughing softly. He waited to see what Coyote would do.

Coyote sat and watched the cheese closely. Minutes passed, then hours. The moon moved in the sky. The cheese moved

Fox tricks Coyote

slowly from the center of the pond to the far shore. Coyote grew anxious. The water on the far side was very deep.

"Where is Fox with that net?" he wondered. "Soon the cheese will escape!"

Sure enough, it looked as though the cheese would slip beneath the far edge of the pond. Coyote could stand it no longer. He leapt into the water and swam after the cheese.

When Coyote reached the edge of the pond, he began trying to grab the cheese. Wherever Coyote grabbed, the cheese seemed to disappear. He thought it must be sinking below his hands. Desperately he tried to dive after it. He dived straight to the bottom of the pond. He still couldn't grab it.

Again and again Coyote dived to the muddy bottom and came up gasping with only mud in his hands.

All this time, Fox had been watching Coyote from his hiding spot. Now he began to laugh so hard that he fell out from behind the bushes.

Seeing Fox, Coyote howled, "Quick, Brother Fox! The cheese has nearly escaped beneath the edge of the pond! Bring the net!"

Sure enough, the cheese disappeared.

Weak from laughing, Fox stood up and said, "You must indeed be starving, Coyote. You've been chasing the moon's reflection for your supper!" Then he ran off into the forest. Coyote went home hungry, wet, and cold.

1. Why did Coyote let Fox go?
2. What was it that Coyote thought was a cheese?
3. What did Coyote find at the bottom of the pond?

Pedro the Rascal

Pedro is a popular legendary character of Mexico. Like the trickster Fox, he outwits others to get what he wants. Pedro's greed is as large as his conscience is small. However, the people he steals from are usually even greedier than he is.

Pedro was always thinking up ways to get the coins from another man's pocket into his own.

He was once walking along with five coins jingling in his pocket. Never mind how they came to rest there. Let's just say it wasn't by honest work. The tune those coins made in Pedro's pocket gave him an idea.

"I'll bet I can make this little crop of money grow," he thought.

Pedro sat down in the shade of a tree beside the road and got out his coins. He made a small hole in each one and tied the coins onto a nearby mesquite bush. Then he sat down beside the bush and waited.

Before long, a prosperous-looking man came riding along. When he saw the gold twinkling in the sun, he stopped his horse.

Pedro's money bush

"What do you have there?" the man asked.

"It's my money bush," Pedro replied.

"What do you mean?" the man questioned.

"Well, sir," Pedro said, "I can see you are a clever fellow, so I'll tell you my secret. This rare bush grows gold coins for me. I was just about to harvest my first crop of money when you came along. Next year, it will grow even more gold."

The man said greedily, "You must sell this bush to me."

At first Pedro said no, but the more he said no, the more the man wanted the bush. Finally Pedro agreed.

"Very well, sir," Pedro said. "You are too clever for me. I'll sell you my money bush for twenty gold coins but only after I have taken my harvest."

Pedro gathered his crop. Then the man paid him the money, and Pedro went on his way. Twenty-five gold coins made his pockets very jingly.

The buyer of the bush waited for his money bush to give him a crop of gold coins. After a year the man realized he had bought a plain old mesquite bush. By then, no one knew where Pedro had gone. Wherever he was, he was most certainly tricking people and stealing from them.

1. *What did Pedro do with his five coins?*
2. *What did Pedro say the bush could do?*
3. *Why didn't Pedro sell the bush as soon as the man asked to buy it?*

A Gift of Seeing

In this tale, told in the state of Jalisco, a man gains fame through deceit. As the story shows, such fame may have a high price.

In the town of Santa Maria lived a man who was a *sabio*, or seer. At least that's what everyone believed. The townspeople thought the sabio had the power to know things that people had done in secret. They also believed he could see into the future and tell what would happen.

Even more useful was the sabio's ability to find things that had been lost. When people could not find something they had lost, they would go to the sabio for help. He would always find the lost object.

The sabio's reputation spread all over the countryside. He could scarcely leave his house without someone pointing him out and saying, "There goes the sabio."

There was something the people didn't know. The man had actually been stealing their things and hiding them. After waiting a while, he would find the things and pretend his magical powers had helped him.

For a long while, the man went on deceiving people. Then one day a group of outlaws came into town. As the men sat in the cantina, they argued about the sabio. One of them believed he had great power. Another believed he was a fake.

"There's a way to find out," suggested one man. "We could kill a goose and bury it in back of the cantina. If the sabio is a real sabio, he will know what we have buried there."

Early the next morning the sabio was awakened rudely by a loud rapping on his door.

"Who is it?" he asked.

One of the outlaws said, "There's something in the ground behind the cantina. Since you are a sabio, you should be able to tell what is there."

The sleepy fellow looked at the rough bunch of men. He thought the bed felt very good right then, but he knew these outlaws. It would be crazy to refuse them.

As the sabio and the outlaws walked to the cantina, word spread throughout the town. A crowd gathered behind the cantina. Everyone wanted to know what the sabio would see buried in the ground.

As the sabio walked toward the cantina, he worried about how to get out of this trouble.

"What is buried behind the cantina?" everyone demanded excitedly. "Tell us! Tell us!"

The sabio stroked his chin and said, "I must ask the spirits. Sometimes they take their time about answering, so do not disturb me."

Then he went home. The people left the cantina slowly, discussing the sabio's curious response.

A day passed, then two, then three. The townspeople began to mutter, "Why doesn't he answer?"

People yelled angrily at the sabio's house, "Hey, what's buried out there? You should know by now!"

Then the outlaws came and demanded the sabio's answer. "You have had plenty of time," they said. "Come with us."

Scared to death, the sabio went with them. He still hadn't thought of a trick that would save him. His feet dragged. At last he stood behind the cantina, knees knocking, with the crowd all around him.

"Tell us what is buried here," the outlaws

demanded, "or we'll bury you with it!"

"My number is up," the sabio thought. "I might as well tell the truth."

With his head hanging low, he kicked at the burial spot. "This is it," he mumbled. "My goose is cooked."

This was the sabio's way of saying, "You've found me out. I'm a fraud."

However, all the outlaws heard was the word "goose." They gasped, convinced the sabio had seen the animal they had buried.

"Hurray for the sabio!" the outlaws cheered. "Long may he live!"

Nonetheless, the man gave up his dishonest ways. Such a scare cost him all his desire to be known as a sabio. It would be better to lose his fame, he decided, than his life.

1. *What did the sabio do that made people believe he had real powers?*
2. *How did the outlaws test his powers?*
3. *Why did the outlaws let the sabio have more time to think?*

Pronunciation Guide

Every effort has been made to present native pronunciations of the unusual names in this book. Sometimes experts differed in their opinions, however, or no pronunciation could be found. Also, certain foreign-language sounds were felt to be unpronounceable by today's readers. In these cases, editorial license was exercised in selecting pronunciations.

Key

The letter or letters used to show pronunciation have the following sounds:

a	as in *map* and *glad*
ah	as in *pot* and *cart*
aw	as in *fall* and *lost*
ch	as in *chair* and *child*
e	as in *let* and *care*
ee	as in *feet* and *please*
ey	as in *play* and *face*
g	as in *gold* and *girl*
hy	as in *huge* and *humor*
i	as in *my* and *high*
ih	as in *sit* and *clear*

j	as in *jelly* and *gentle*
k	as in *skill* and *can*
ky	as in *cute*
l	as in *long* and *pull*
my	as in *mule*
ng	as in *sing* and *long*
ny	as in *canyon* and *onion*
o	as in *slow* and *go*
oo	as in *cool* and *move*
ow	as in *cow* and *round*
s	as in *soon* and *cent*
sh	as in *shoe* and *sugar*
th	as in *thin* and *myth*
u	as in *put* and *look*
uh	as in *run* and *up*
y	as in *you* and *yesterday*
z	as in *zoo* and *pairs*

Guide

Capital letters are used to represent stressed syllables. For example, the word *ugly* would be written here as "UHG lee."

Aztec: AZ tek

basilisk: BAS uh LISK

Chac: CHAHK

charro: CHAH ro

Chinantec: chin AHN tek

Homshuk: HOHM shook

Huichol: wee CHOL

Hurakan: hoo rah KAHN

Ixtlaccihuatl: ES tuh lah SEE waht uhl

Jalisco: hah LEES ko

Maya: MAH yah

Mazatec: MAHZ uh tek

mesquite: mes KEET

nagual: nah GWAHL

Nayarit: nah yah REET

Oaxaca: wah HAH kah

Olmec: OHL mek

plantain: PLAN tin

Popoluca: po po LOO kah

Popocatepetl: po PO kah TEH pet uhl

Popol Vuh: PO pul VOO

Pueblo: poo EB lo

Quetzalcoatl: kets sahl KO ah tuhl

Quintana Roo: keen TAH nuh RO o

sabio: SAH bee o

Santa Maria: SAHN ta mah REE ah

Seri: SEH ree

Sierra Madre: see ER ah MAH drey

Shoé-pi-tou-tou-tou: sho AY pee too too too

Sonora: so NOR ah

Tezcatlipoca: tez caht lee POH kah

Tzotzil: TSOT seel

Vera Cruz: VER uh KROOZ

Yaqui: YAH kee

Yucatan: YOO kah TAHN

Zapotecan: ZAH puh TEHK uhn